W9-AKD-949

Date Due

AUG 27 1970			
OCT 26 1970			
OCT 11 '72			
MAR 23 1976			
SEP. 9 1982			
JA 1 1 '89			
AG 0 2 '91			
FEB 15 '94			
SEP 8 '94			
AG 23 '99			
SE 22 '00			
OC 1 9 '09			
OC 0 8 '20			

Demco 38-297

j
910.9
F

9007

Foster, Genevieve
Year of Columbus 1492

EAU CLAIRE DISTRICT LIBRARY

1492 ** 1492 ** 1492
1492 ** 1492 ** 1492 ** 1492
Fourteen Hundred
Ninety Two
Columbus
sailed
the Ocean blue
1492
1492 ** 1492 ** 1492

1492 ** 1492 ** 1492
Fourteen Hundred
Ninety Two
Columbus
sailed
the Ocean blue
1492
1492 ** 1492 ** 1492

1492 ** 1492 ** 1492
1492 ** 1492 ** 1492 ** 1492 ** 1492
Fourteen Hundred
Ninety Two
Columbus
sailed
the Ocean blue
1492
1492 ** 1492 ** 1492

YEAR OF COLUMBUS 1492

by Genevieve Foster

Charles Scribner's Sons New York

Baker and Taylor 6/29/70 - 3 44
EAU CLAIRE DISTRICT LIBRARY
9007
81420

Copyright © 1969 Genevieve Foster

This book published simultaneously in the United States of America and in Canada—Copyright under the Berne Convention. All rights reserved. No part of this book may be reproduced in any form without the permission of Charles Scribner's Sons.

A-9.69{RZ}

Printed in the United States of America
Library of Congress Catalog Card Number 77-85268

CONTENTS

Part One
THE
COLUMBUS
STORY
John II
Isabella
Vasco da Gama

THE YEAR WAS 1492. It was the twelfth day of October. The sun had just risen and was shining softly down upon a small coral island in the Atlantic Ocean. Christopher Columbus stood on the shore holding in his hand the staff of a large, bright-colored flag. Soon he was planting it in the warm sand to show that the island now belonged to the King and Queen of Spain, Ferdinand and Isabella.

Columbus did not know where the island was. Not exactly. He hoped and believed that it was near the coast of China, or, better still, not far from India. He would then have glorious news for Queen Isabella. He would have done what he had assured her could be done, which was to reach India by sailing west around the world.

For many years the King of Portugal had been trying to reach India by sailing south round the end of Africa. Columbus had persuaded Queen Isabella to let him try sailing west across the Atlantic Ocean. Although it was a daring chance to take, the queen had furnished Columbus with money and ships to try out his idea.

It was a good idea, a brave and wonderful idea. And it might have succeeded if there had been nothing but ocean between Spain and India. That is what all the scholars believed. No one, not even the wisest men in Spain, had the slightest suspicion that far out in the ocean there was a huge body of land blocking the way to India, a tremendous continent, bigger by far than all the countries of Europe put together. But there it was!

And there was Columbus, on this bright October morning, planting the Spanish flag on a small island off the coast of a New World which he had discovered quite by accident. He had discovered what was to be called America, but to the end of his life, Columbus himself never knew it. He made four voyages across the ocean, sailing in and out among the islands which lie between the Atlantic Ocean and the Caribbean Sea. He was so sure that they were near India that he called the people living on them Indians, and we still call them the West Indies.

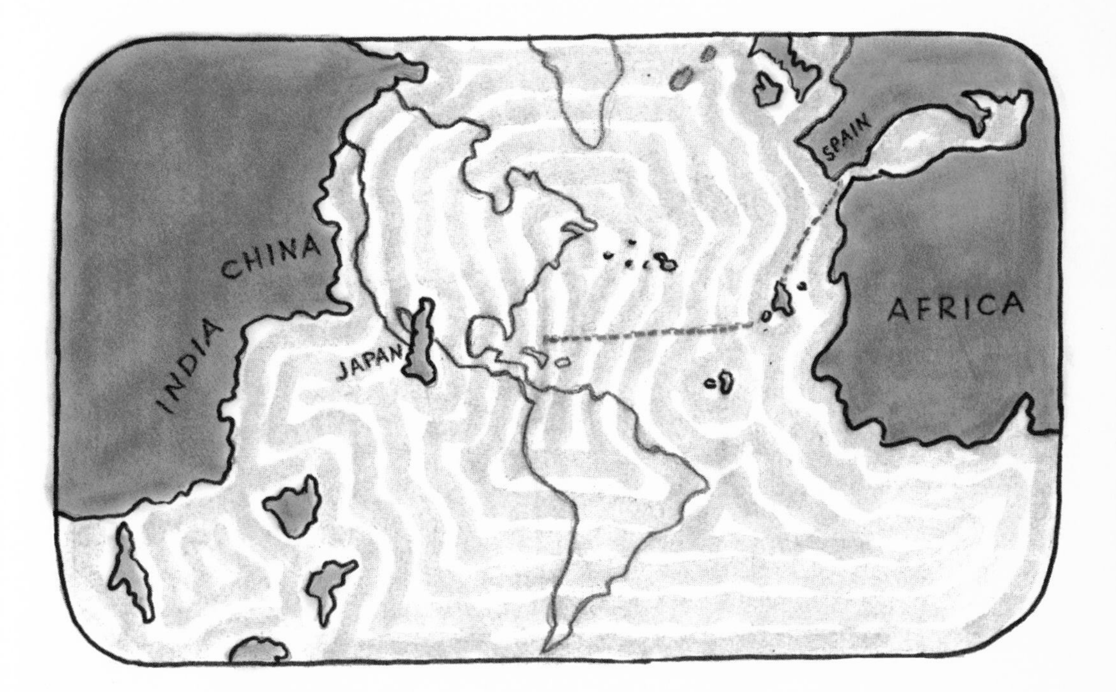

THIS IS JOHN II, King of Portugal, such a good king that his people called him "John the Perfect." In 1492, John II had been king of Portugal for eleven years. All that time he had been trying to reach India by going down around the end of Africa. That was the route which had been chosen by his great-uncle, Prince Henry the Navigator, who had dreamed of finding a new sea route to India long before King John and Christopher Columbus were born.

Finding a new way to India really meant finding a way to the land that pepper came from. That is what Prince Henry

Portugal

had been hoping to find. He had wanted to get pepper and other spices without having to buy them from the Arabs.

Arab merchants were the only ones who had pepper for sale, because only the Arabs knew the way to India. From that fabulous land Arab traders brought back rare jewels and precious treasures to be sold in all the city ports along the eastern end of the Mediterranean.

Of all the treasures which the Arabs had to offer, spices were most in demand. And of all the spices, pepper was the most valuable. People had no refrigerators in those days, no way of keeping meat fresh. Pepper covered up the taste of half spoiled meat and made it fit to eat. Everyone in Spain,

1. Lisbon　　2. Calicut

Portugal and all the other countries of Europe clamored for pepper, but the Arabs kept the price so high that only the very rich could afford to buy it.

The Arabs had a short, easy route to India. Just across the Indian Ocean lay the harbor of Calicut. There the Arabs loaded their spice ships and sailed them to the tip of the Red Sea. From there the spices went by camel caravan to the Mediterranean. The Arabs kept their route well guarded. They wanted no rivals sharing the rich trade.

Prince Henry knew that the Portuguese would have to find another way to India. He had no idea, of course, when he sent out his first explorers, how huge Africa was or how many years it would take them just to reach the end of the continent. When his life ended, the Portuguese explorers were but halfway down the African coast.

Prince Henry the Navigator died in 1460. King John was only five years old. Christopher Columbus was nine. That is when this story of 1492 begins.

CHRISTOPHER COLUMBUS lived in the Italian seaport of Genoa when he was a boy. He was then called Cristoforo Colombo by everyone he knew.

Genoa, where he was born, was both a city and a state, one of the tiny nations into which Italy was then divided.

1451 Genoa

Father Colombo was a weaver. As soon as Christopher and his younger brother Bartholomew were old enough, they were being taught their father's trade, though neither of them wanted to be a weaver. Bartholomew would rather draw maps than card wool. Christopher longed to be a sailor. Both were in their teens when their wishes came true.

Christopher went to sea on one of the merchant ships of Genoa and began sailing back and forth across the Mediterranean, learning navigation.

Bartholomew went to work as a map maker in Lisbon, the capital and seaport of Portugal. By 1474 he had his own map shop. One day, as he was drawing, he heard the heavy door creak open. He looked up. There, to his great surprise, stood his brother Christopher! What a joyful reunion!

Columbus stayed on in Lisbon to work in the map shop with Bartholomew. But drawing maps made him restless. When the chance came, he went on a short voyage to the North Atlantic. After that he began to dream of sailing much farther out upon the Atlantic Ocean, possibly around the world. Why not? All scholars agreed that the world was round. Every map showed the land as a single island surrounded by one big ocean. So why was it not possible to sail

from one side of the island to the other—that is, from Portugal to China?

Bartholomew thought that it might be done, provided the ocean that separated them was not too wide. That was the big question. How wide was the ocean? No one knew.

About two years after his return to Lisbon, Columbus married a young Portuguese lady, Dona Felipe. The next year, 1480, their son Diego was born. They were then living

Portugal

on one of the Madeira Islands out about two hundred miles in the Atlantic Ocean. There Columbus saw pieces of old wood that had floated in from the west. They were so well carved that he felt sure they must have come from islands off the coast of India or China. If so, surely the ocean could not be too wide for the voyage he wanted to make.

In the year 1481, John II became king of Portugal. Hoping to carry out the plan of his great-uncle, he began building a new fort on the African coast.

Columbus paid a visit to the fort, going there on a ship that had stopped at the Madeira Islands on its way from Lisbon. The coast where the fort was built was called the Gold Coast, because of the rich gold mines that had been found there. As Columbus saw the Portuguese captains loading their ships with gold, he was sure King John would find it hard to make any of them go farther on, hunting for India. So why, thought Columbus, would not King John be glad to let him try his plan for reaching India by sailing west across the Atlantic Ocean?

Columbus still did not know how wide the ocean was. The books he read did not agree. As soon as he returned to Portugal, he wrote to a famous Italian astronomer, whose answer delighted him. The ocean between Portugal and China, said this astronomer, was not very wide—only about 5,000 miles. Thrilled, excited and full of hope, Columbus went to see the King. He made his plan sound so marvelous that King John was ready to finance the voyage if his councillors agreed. They did not. They declared that such a voyage was impossible, just a crazy man's dream. It was 10,000 miles to China, not 5,000. That would mean sailing three months on the open ocean. It was impossible, utterly impossible!

They were wrong, absolutely wrong, Columbus said to his brother. And he would prove it. Some other king would surely furnish him with ships. Why not the King and Queen of Spain? They had no gold mines in Africa. They should be glad of a way to beat the Portuguese to the land of spices. Bartholomew agreed, and so in 1485 Columbus left for Spain. Diego was only five, and as his mother had died, he sailed to Spain with his father. Their ship anchored in the Spanish harbor of Palos. As Columbus was wondering how he could meet the queen and who would take care of Diego, he looked up. There on a hill above the harbor he saw a monastery, where both of his problems were soon to be solved.

Fray Juan Perez, the kindly friar, welcomed the small boy. And after hearing Columbus explain his marvelous idea, he said that he knew the Queen well and would be more than glad to write to her and arrange for a meeting.

Queen Isabella was then in Cordova. Because Columbus had to travel on mule back from Palos to Cordova, he arrived there too late. The royal family and the court had gone away for the winter and would not return until spring. There was nothing for Columbus to do but to wait.

QUEEN ISABELLA RECEIVED COLUMBUS for the first time on a May morning in 1486. She was stirred by the enthusiasm of this unknown Italian and his strange plan. She promised to appoint a committee of scholars to study it. What pleased her the most was that Columbus wished to carry the Christian religion to natives across the sea. She and the King were then waging what they called a "holy war" to drive out all Mohammedans living in Spain and make it a country for Christians only.

In the fall, Columbus explained his plan to the committee and began to wait hopefully for their approval. Four years went by, and he was still waiting. At long last, the scholars advised the Queen "not to favor an affair which appeared impossible to any educated person, however little learning he might have."

Feeling sorry for Columbus, Isabella said that if he wished to wait until the war was over, he might present his plan again. She would then have more time to think about it.

More time? thought Columbus. No indeed! He would go back now to Portugal and talk to his brother about presenting the plan to either the King of England or the King of France. He stopped at the monastery to call for Diego. There the good friar persuaded him to wait. After all, the war could not last long. The Mohammedans would soon have to surrender.

It was true. On January 2, 1492, Ferdinand and Isabella celebrated their victory. A few days later they sent for Columbus. They told him that they had definitely decided not to finance his voyage. They bade him farewell. He bowed and departed. As Columbus was riding out of the city on his mule, the King's Treasurer, in amazement, rushed to the Queen. He begged her not to let Columbus leave. Consider what a disgrace it would be to her if some other king were to gain the riches that should have belonged to Spain! A messenger went galloping down the road, caught up with Columbus, and brought him back.

By spring, Columbus had a document, signed by Queen Isabella and the King, appointing him, Cristóbal Colón, their Admiral of the Ocean Sea and governor of whatever islands he might discover on his voyage to India. He was also to have a share of the riches to be gained in spices and gold.

THE NINA, THE PINTA, THE SANTA MARIA sailed from the harbor of Palos at the end of summer, 1492. On board the three small ships were ninety men who had signed up for this peculiar voyage. As the shore line faded away, none of them felt sure that he would ever see it again.

By the time they had sailed several days beyond the Canary Islands, they knew that they were farther away from land than any man had ever been before. What if they should sail so far over the curve of the world that they could never get back? No ship could sail uphill! Why had they let this crazy

Italian persuade them to go on such a mad voyage? They remembered all the horrible tales about sea monsters that could overturn a ship or swallow it whole.

Who was this Cristóbal Colón, this so-called Admiral who promised them gold in a land they would not live to see? What they should do if he would not turn back was to throw him overboard. Yet when they threatened to do it, he faced them with courage and showed that he was a brave man. And he was a good navigator. No one of them could deny that.

For thirty days they had seen nothing but water. Then, as Columbus pointed out, they kept seeing small birds and other signs that land must be near.

One day a branch with red berries floated by. And a day or so later, a carved stick.

Then at dawn, one Friday, after thirty-five days at sea, they saw an island. Thanks be to God!

Men in three small rowboats went ashore, fell to their knees, and kissed the ground with tears of joy.

Columbus christened the island San Salvador, and soon he was planting a flag in the sand, claiming this island which he had discovered now belonged to the King and Queen of Spain, Ferdinand and Isabella.

This map shows the tiny island where Columbus landed. At first sight of his ships, the natives came running to the shore to see what kind of huge birds had flown in from the sea. They were pleased with the beads and trinkets the Spaniards had brought, and in return offered parrots, skeins of cotton thread, and whatever else they had to give.

Columbus was delighted. "All I have to do now is to look for gold and spices," he wrote that night in his journal. The coast of China, he was sure, could not be far away, nor Japan with its golden temples, nor the harbors of India, filled with fragrant spices. The next weeks he spent sailing in and out among the islands. Though there were no spices to be found, there was gold on the island of Haiti. Much gold, the Indians told Columbus, was to be found in the center of the island. This joyful news helped him to bear the loss of his flag ship.

Christmas Eve, the *Santa Maria* was wrecked on the rocky shore of Haiti and had to be abandoned. All Christmas day the Indians worked, carrying its beams and timbers ashore. With this wood, they helped Columbus build Fort Navidad, the first Spanish fort in the New World.

Later when Columbus was ready to leave on the return voyage to Spain, forty men were glad to be left behind at the fort and begin searching for gold.

Now came days of triumph for Columbus, the most glorious days of his life. He landed at Seville and went from there to Barcelona to see the King and Queen. His journey across Spain was one continuous celebration. At every town the mayor and council came out to welcome him. All along the way people flocked to see the remarkable man who had crossed the great ocean and returned alive. They stared at the red-brown Indians he had brought with him, marveled at the bright-colored birds they carried and at their golden ornaments.

AT BARCELONA the entire court turned out to welcome the hero. As Columbus knelt to kiss the hands of the King and Queen, Ferdinand and Isabella rose from their thrones and, as a special honor, bade him be seated with them while they questioned him about his voyage and discovery.

For his services they made him a nobleman. He was now to be Don (or Lord) Cristóbal Colón. And his new coat of arms was to bear the royal symbols, the golden castle and the purple lion, as well as anchors of a ship and the islands of the New World he had discovered for Spain.

IN 1492 THE PORTUGUESE were still searching for their sea route to India. In 1488 they had found the end of Africa, calling it the Cape of Good Hope, but it was another ten years before that hope of landing in India actually came true. Then on May 22, 1498, the Portuguese explorer Vasco da Gama sailed into the busy harbor of Calicut.

India

The ruler of Calicut was called the Samorin, or Lord of the Sea. He protected the Arab merchants who dealt in spices and was so well paid by them that he was immensely wealthy. One spring day a messenger arrived at the Samorin's palace to tell of three strange looking ships in the harbor from a place called Portugal.

A few days later Vasco da Gama appeared with a letter from his king and also a few gifts.

"Most powerful ruler of India," he said, making a deep bow, "the great King of Portugal, my master, has heard of your fame and wishes to exchange goods of his country for those of yours, especially spices."

The Arab councillor resented this rival trader and was not pleased when the Samorin took the King's letter and pressed it to his breast as a sign of friendship.

The next time Vasco da Gama came to the palace, the Arab merchants had him seized by the palace guards. When he threatened to sink all the ships in the harbor and turn his guns on the city if they did not release him, the Arab councillor advised the Samorin to have the foreigner put to death. The Samorin, however, followed the opposite advice of his Indian councillor and allowed the stranger to depart unharmed.

Vasco da Gama, thankful to escape alive, loaded his ships with spices and sailed for home. And so the first spice ships from India entered the harbor of Lisbon. The sea route to India had been found. The great dream of Prince Henry the Navigator had at last come true.

Copernicus
Part Two
ARTISTS
AND
SCIENTISTS
Michelangelo
Leonardo

The Universe

according to Ptolemy
The seven planets revolve around the earth inside a band of fixed stars called the Zodiac.

IF THE IDEAS people in 1492 had about geography seem strange, their notions about sun, moon, stars, and planets seem even stranger. For one thing, they were sure that the earth was the center of the universe and that the sun revolved around it. The man who discovered their mistake and declared that the earth revolved around the sun was Nicolaus Copernicus. Copernicus is a name to be remembered. Astronauts exploring outer space, all the wonders of modern astronomy, began with Copernicus.

Copernicus

Copernicus was born in Poland in 1473, just one year before Columbus first went to Portugal. Mikolaj Kopernik was his name in Polish. From the time he was a small boy he loved to watch the stars. On cold, clear nights they were so marvelously brilliant. He knew the names of the seven planets: Sun, Moon, Mars, Jupiter, Mercury, Venus, and Saturn. He longed to know more about them and how they moved around the earth. Yet when he grew older, he could not make himself believe what he was being taught.

At the University of Poland he studied from a book written by a famous old astronomer named Ptolemy.

Ptolemy said that the earth was the center of the universe and stood absolutely still. The sky was solid like a platter. There were seven planets. These were fastened to the platter, which kept turning around.

But how could that be? thought Copernicus. If all the planets were fastened to the same thing, they would travel around at the same speed. And they did not. He had watched them in the sky enough to know that. Something must be wrong somewhere.

Italy was then the great center of learning. Nicolaus persuaded his uncle, who was a bishop, to send him to an

Italian university. He promised to study medicine, law, and mathematics, as well as astronomy.

In a lecture he heard one of the professors say that the ancient Greeks had doubted that the earth was the center of the universe or that it stood still. That was the starting point for Copernicus. Exciting questions went whirling through his mind.

If the earth moved, what about the sun? Did the sun stand still? If so, why did it seem to rise and set? Somehow he must find the answers to these questions.

After he returned to Poland, Copernicus continued to study the movements of the planets. He tested what he saw by the use of mathematics. He found some of the answers to his questions, but he was never satisfied that he had discovered all that he could. He worked and studied as long as he lived. Just before he died, he wrote a small book, which is now very famous. In it he said:

> The earth is not the center of the Universe.
>
> All the planets revolve around the sun. We revolve around the sun like any other planet.
>
> Therefore the SUN is the center of the Universe.

THESE DRAWINGS of a bird's wing, a helicopter, and a parachute are copied from those made in the days of Columbus by a man who was five hundred years ahead of his

Leonardo

time in believing that men should be able to fly. This man was Leonardo da Vinci. He was born in the city-state of Florence in 1452, just one year after Columbus had been born in Genoa.

Leonardo had so many talents and interests that it is hard to know whether to call him a painter, a sculptor, an engineer, a scientist, an inventor, or a philosopher. Actually, he was all of these.

The drawings are from one of his notebooks, in which he jotted down things he saw and thought he wanted to remember. All were put down helter skelter, waiting for the day when he had time to sort them out and put them in order. He never had time. The world was too full of fascinating things to see and do and think and wonder about.

Leonardo was left-handed and all the pages in his notebooks were written from right to left. This is called mirror writing. Hold this sentence up to a mirror and you will see why.

The earth is a star
much like the moon.

Although Leonardo grew up and studied in Florence, he spent much of his life in Milan. There he lived at the court of the duke who ruled the city-state of Milan.

Leonardo did whatever the duke desired. That meant all kinds of things, from painting portraits of lovely ladies to designing machines for dredging harbors and canals. He decorated rooms in the castle. He designed costumes and scenery for pageants and plays. For many years he worked on a statue of the duke's father seated on horseback, which was to be placed in the palace courtyard.

Leonardo had lived in Milan for over ten years when he was asked to decorate the end of the dining hall in a monastery which was not far from the palace of the duke. There he painted his great masterpiece, "The Last Supper."

This shows the twelve disciples having the last meal they were ever to share with their teacher and master, Jesus of Nazareth. The next day, on a hill outside of Jerusalem, Jesus was to be crucified and die on a cross. But his disciples believed that he rose to life again and that he would also save them from death. So they called him the Saviour, or Christ. His life and teaching grew into the religion known as Christianity.

HERE IS MICHELANGELO, one of the world's great artists, carving his name on his first famous statue, the "Pietà." Michelangelo Buonarotti was born in 1475 in the city of Florence, the art center of Italy. When he was fourteen, he attracted the attention of the great Lorenzo de' Medici, who was the powerful ruler of the city-state of Florence.

Michelangelo

Lorenzo "the Magnificent," as he was called, was a great lover of art. In his palace he had established a school of painting and sculpture. There especially gifted boys, recommended by their teachers, were invited to study. One of these young art students was Michelangelo.

One morning Lorenzo happened to see the boy carving the head of a faun, asked him his name, and sent for his father.

"You have a gifted son," said Lorenzo. "I am inviting him to live here as one of my family, to study and become a sculptor. One day he will do honor to us all and to Florence."

The three sons of Lorenzo, who were about Michelangelo's age, soon discovered that though he was talented, he was not easy to live with. One day they saw that a classmate whom he had been teasing too much had hit him and broken his nose. That is why it looks crooked in his portrait.

In 1492, just a few months before Columbus discovered the New World, Lorenzo de' Medici died. Michelangelo was heartbroken and fled from the palace. He thought that Piero, the oldest son, who would now take his father's place, had always been jealous of him and would probably drive him out. Michelangelo was surprised. Piero, who was foolish and unpredictable, sent for him to come back. In January, 1494, there had been a tremendous snow storm, and he wanted Michelangelo to make a snow man in the palace courtyard.

Two years later Michelangelo was on his way to Rome, where he was to spend many years of his life. He had been sent for by a cardinal. This churchman had discovered that a statue of Cupid which he had purchased in Rome had been made in Florence by a young sculptor named Michelangelo.

In the summer of 1498, this little-known sculptor from Florence signed a contract for the statue that was to make him famous. He agreed to show the Virgin Mary, the mother of Jesus, holding the dead Christ in her arms and to have it done in one year. Choosing a large block of pure white marble, Michelangelo began to carve it and, following what he called "the heart's image," made something incredibly beautiful. The "Pietà," when finished, was placed in the old church of St. Peter's. There, one day, Michelangelo was shocked to overhear a group of visitors declaring that it must be the work of a certain sculptor of Milan. Slipping back later, he carved his name on the belt of the Virgin. It is the only work of painting or sculpture that Michelangelo ever signed. And he lived to be eighty-nine.

THIS IS A STATUE which Michelangelo made of Moses, the great Hebrew prophet of ancient times. It was Moses who led his people, the Israelites, out of slavery in Egypt. That flight was known as the Exodus. In 1492 there was another exodus of Jewish people—from Spain. In April, just two weeks before Ferdinand and Isabella signed the agreement with Columbus, they signed a decree against the Spanish Jews. The Jews were given a choice. Either they must accept the Christian religion or leave the country by the end of the summer. This was a terrible blow to the Jews, who had lived in Spain for many hundreds of years.

Why had the King and Queen of Spain signed this decree? For the same reason that they had fought the Mohammedans. They wanted to make Spain a completely Christian country.

This exodus was a sad loss for Spain. The King's Treasurer, who had persuaded Queen Isabella to finance Columbus, was a Jew, as were many high officials at court. Doctors, lawyers, scholars, bankers, many of the most highly educated people in Spain were driven out of the country.

Some of them went to Portugal, a few to North Africa, others to Italy. Most fortunate were those who reached Turkey. They were welcomed by the Sultan. Though he himself was a Mohammedan, he was delighted to have these fine scholars and scientists enrich his country with their skills, regardless of their religion. He had little respect for the Spanish rulers who had driven them out.

Emperor of China
Part Three
AROUND THE WORLD
King of Ethiopia
The Aztec Montezuma
The Topa Inca

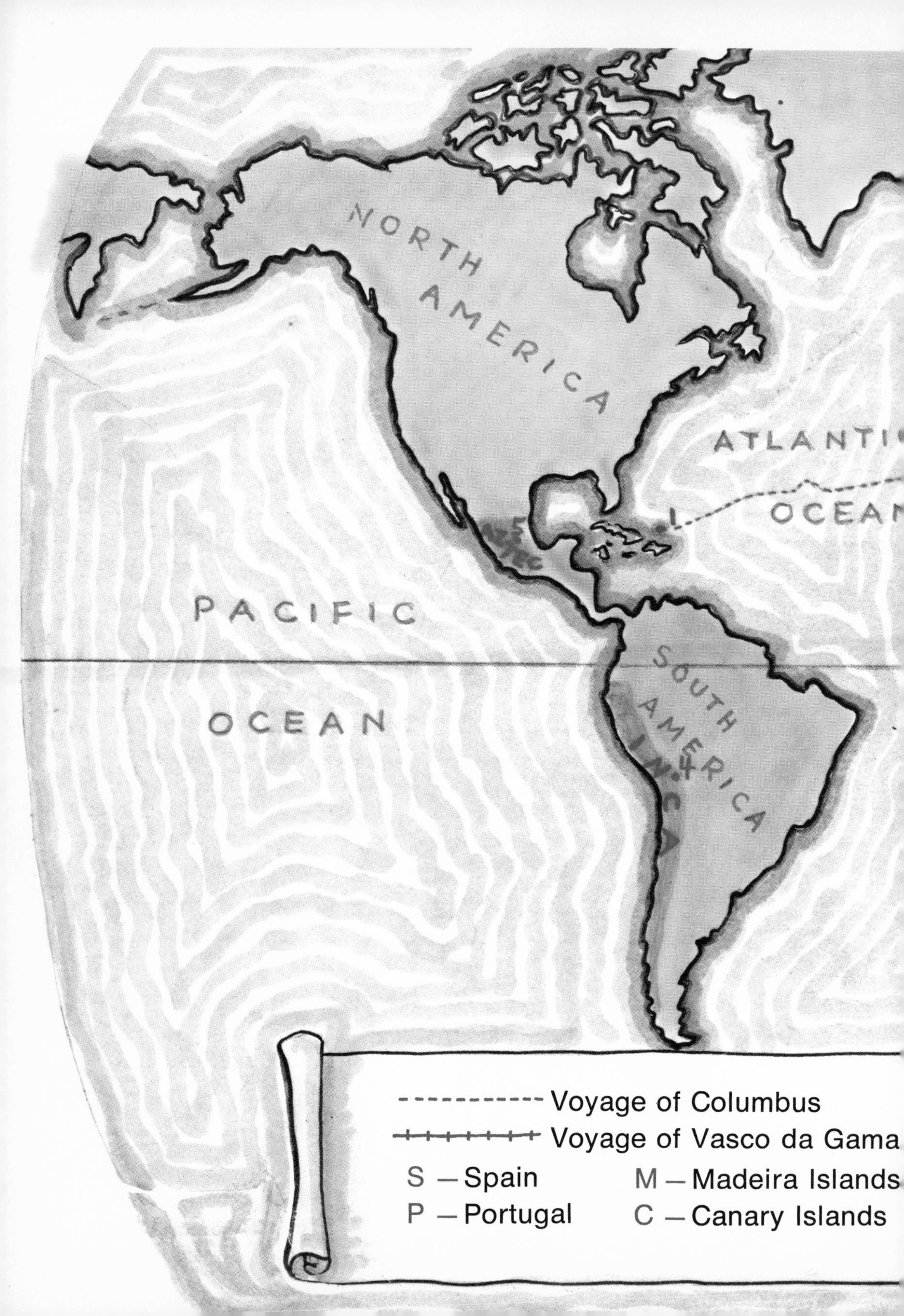
NORTH AMERICA
1
5
PACIFIC
OCEAN
SOUTH AMERICA
INCA
4
Voyage of Columbus
Voyage of Vasco da Gama
S — Spain
P — Portugal
M — Madeira Islands
C — Canary Islands

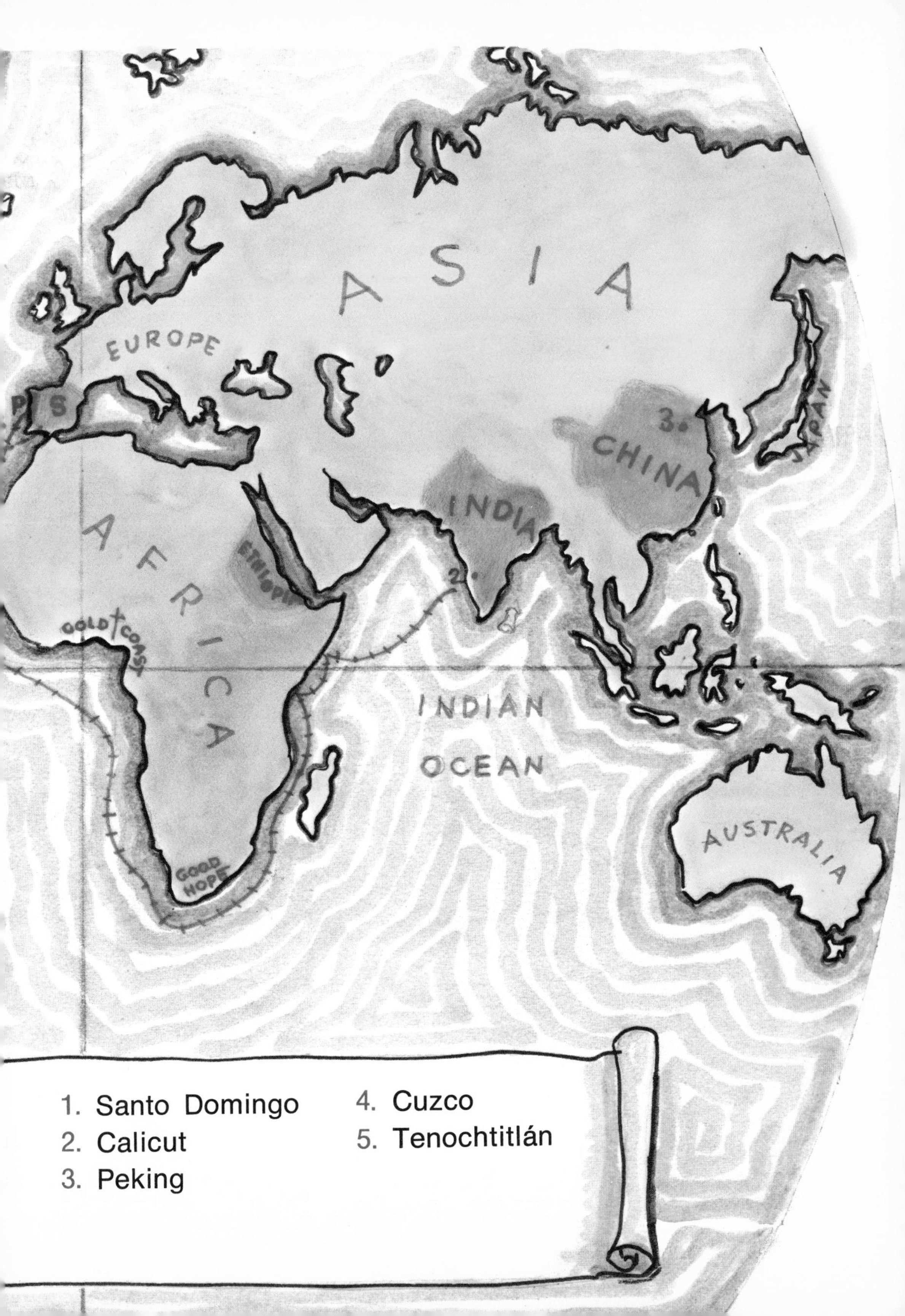
ASIA
EUROPE
P
S
AFRICA
ETHIOPIA
GOLD COAST
GOOD HOPE
INDIA
2.
CHINA
3.
INDIAN
OCEAN
AUSTRALIA
1. Santo Domingo
2. Calicut
3. Peking
4. Cuzco
5. Tenochtitlán

IN AFRICA, IN 1492, there was a king who belonged to the oldest royal family in the world. He ruled a country south of Egypt, which was called Ethiopia, from a Greek word meaning "dark skinned." From early times Ethiopia had been a Christian country. But for almost a thousand years it had been cut off from all other Christian countries by the Mohammedans, who had conquered Egypt. Ethiopia had been lost and forgotten.

King John of Portugal, however, had an idea that somewhere in Africa there was a mysterious Christian king named Prester John. In 1487 he sent a man named Couilhã to hunt for this king, hoping that the king might help the Portuguese in getting to India for spices. This was a dangerous

Ethiopia

mission because the hostile Arabs wanted no competition in the spice trade. To travel through Egypt, Couilhã disguised himself as an Arab merchant selling honey.

In 1492 he finally reached Ethiopia. There, instead of Prester John he found a king called "The Conquering Lion of Judah," whose ancestor, the first royal ruler of this land, had been the son of King Solomon and the Queen of Sheba.

The king was so overjoyed to have an ambassador from the outside world appear at his lonely court that he kept him year after year, refusing to let him leave. At last, with no hope of ever returning to his family in Portugal, Couilhã chose a beautiful Ethiopian woman to be his wife and had a second family of sons and daughters.

"ALL THAT IS UNDER HEAVEN." That was the Chinese name for China. That is what every Chinese emperor believed his rich and beautiful country to be. The characters alongside the portrait of the emperor spell "Ming."

China

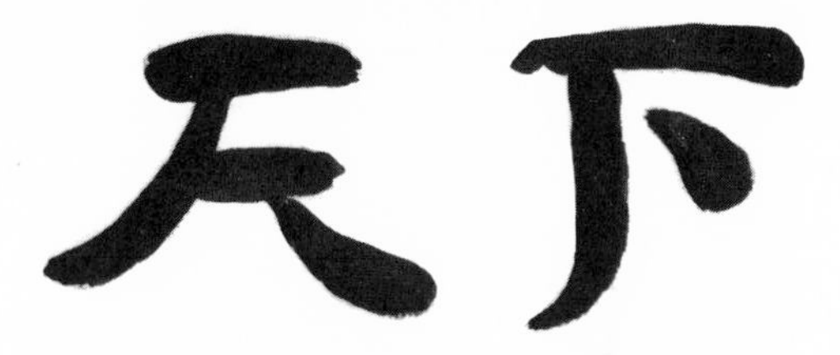

That was the name of the dynasty, or ruling family, to which the emperor belonged. The Mings had begun to rule the year Columbus was born. In 1492 the ninth Ming emperor, Hung Chi, sat on the red dragon throne in the imperial city of Peking.

Peking was actually three cities in one. Walls forty feet high and as wide on top as a street surrounded the outer city, where the common people lived and worked. Another wall enclosed the smaller middle city, where ministers, scholars and government officials had their homes and offices. Inside of that was a still smaller "Forbidden City," walled about and strictly guarded. This held the beautiful palaces and spacious gardens of the Emperor. There, safe and secure, Hung Chi, the Son of Heaven, dwelt in peace and contentment, observing the time-honored customs of this most ancient nation on earth, then over 4,000 years old.

Hung Chi was not at all curious about the barbarians who might be living elsewhere in the world. Had he known that the Portuguese and Spanish were so eager to get to China, he would not have been surprised. All barbarians wished to share in the riches of his country. All the rulers round about sent tribute to the emperor of China. Ambassadors kow-towed before him, touching their foreheads to the ground. Traders came from far away to buy the beautiful porcelains, the lacquer ware, and precious carving of ivory and jade.

For centuries China had been the great center of learning in Asia. All neighboring people had learned from the Chinese, especially those in the nearby island kingdom of Japan. More books had been written and printed in Chinese than in all other languages of the world put together.

Most honored among the books were those which contained the wisdom of the great teacher Confucius, who had lived in China about 500 B.C.

About the time that Confucius lived in China, there had lived a prince in India called the Buddha. His teachings became a religion known as Buddhism. This religion spread to China and from there to Japan, the small island kingdom to the east which the Chinese called "The Land of the Rising Sun."

IN JAPAN, just six years before Leonardo da Vinci began to paint "The Last Supper," a great religious painting was made by a Buddhist priest whose name was Sesshu. It is a landscape painted on a long scroll. This landscape, like "The Last Supper," is one of the world's famous paintings. And, like Leonardo da Vinci, the painter Sesshu was not only a great painter but a man of many talents.

As a small boy it is said that he was so high-spirited and hard to manage that his mother sent him to be trained by priests in a temple of Zen. Zen is a form of Buddhism. One day, according to the myth, Sesshu had been so unruly that he was tied to one of the temple posts. He cried so hard that the tears fell to his feet. Using tears for ink, he drew a rat in the dust. The drawing was so perfect that the rat came to life, gnawed through the ropes, and set the boy free.

At twenty, Sesshu was himself a priest in the temple at Kyoto. There, at the court of the emperor, he often acted

as host to foreign ambassadors. From there he was sent on an important trading mission to China.

On his return from China, Sesshu painted his famous "Landscape Scroll." He said that though he had learned much from the Chinese painters, his true teachers were rivers and mountains, not men. In the painting, we see how small the men are next to the mountains, trees and rivers. Sesshu is showing how people are related to the world around them. Within all living things there is the same great eternal Spirit of Life. Knowing this, no man can think himself better or more important than any other person or living thing.

That is a belief held by the followers of Zen.

Side by side with Buddhism, which had been brought from China, the Japanese held to their own early religion, known as Shinto. This began with the worship of the Sun Goddess and of her grandson, who had been their first emperor. In 1492 the emperor of Japan was still worshipped as a god—the grandchild of the Sun.

Far across the Pacific from Japan, in the high mountains facing the same ocean, were two other empires of the Sun. Their rulers were also said to be children of the Sun. These were the Incas and the Aztecs.

SUNRISE IN JAPAN was sunset in Peru, land of the Incas. There in the high Andes, 11,000 feet above the sea, was Cuzco, "City of the Sun," capital of an empire larger than that of China. It lay along the western coast of South America from Ecuador to Chile.

The emperor, known as the Inca, was worshipped as a god in a Temple to the Sun, whose walls were covered with sheets of gold. All the temples and palaces of Cuzco were

built of huge interlocking stones and decorated with gold. Gold was everywhere to be seen and everywhere to be found in this shining land. The Incas called it "Sweat of the Sun."

The Inca empire was held together by good roads. Roads zigzagged up the mountain peaks, ran along the high ridges and over steep ravines on swaying bridges. All the roads were narrow since the only travelers were men on foot or llamas carrying baggage. The Incas had no wheeled carts, no horses, only the sure-footed llama.

In 1492, this empire of the Incas was probably the most highly organized and perfectly managed nation in the entire world. The two emperors who had made it so were Pachacuti Inca and his son Topa Inca.

Pachacuti, who was the conqueror and founder of the empire, began to rule about thirteen years before Columbus was born. He was not only a victorious general, conquering all the warring tribes surrounding Cuzco; he was also a most wise and skillful statesman. Often he could persuade a tribe to join the empire willingly, in order to enjoy its benefits of peace and prosperity. Topa Inca extended the empire to its final boundaries and perfected the government established by his father.

Leaders of each newly conquered tribe were obliged to learn the Inca language, known as Quechua, to make sure they understood one another. There was no form of writing, but spoken messages sped along at the rate of one hundred forty miles a day. Runners were stationed along the roads a mile or two apart. As one runner arrived, another stood ready to memorize the message and carry it on.

Inca farmers worked part time on their own land, part time on land owned by the state. Warehouses were stocked with food so that if crops failed no one went hungry. Orphans, invalids and the aged were always fed. But no idlers. Everyone must do what he was able to do, knowing that when he grew too old to work he would be cared for.

Topa Inca died in 1493, just a year after Columbus discovered the New World. The Inca empire was at its peak of perfection. But before long, Spaniards, greedy for gold, would completely destroy that wonderful civilization.

THE HIGH VALLEY OF MEXICO, with its blue lakes and snowy mountain peaks, was the home of the Aztecs. They had invaded and conquered it from the Toltecs, who were a cultured, peaceful people. The Aztecs were both warlike and very religious. All captives taken in war were sacrificed on the altars of their gods, especially the war god.

Huitzilopochtli, the Sorcerer Humming Bird, was the

Aztec

great Aztec god of war. His twin brother, Quetzalcoatl, the Feathered Serpent, was the Toltec god of peace. Both were sons of the Sun, born in the dawn of time. But since war is the enemy of peace, the brothers were enemies.

Quetzalcoatl, god of the Toltecs, had left Mexico before his brother Huitzilopochtli had led the warlike Aztecs into the high valley. But he had made this promise:

"When the time comes, I shall return by way of the eastern sea, together with white and bearded men."

After the Aztecs had defeated the Toltecs, they destroyed the temple of the Feathered Serpent. Then his brother, the war god, told them where to build their city. He said they must find an eagle with a snake in his beak, perched on a cactus on a rock in the middle of a lake.

On that spot the Aztecs built their city, calling it Tenochtitlán, meaning "bear the cactus." In 1492, the city was a little over one hundred years old.

Montezuma II, last of the Aztec emperors, was then about twelve. Ten years later, when he had become the emperor, Columbus was on his last voyage to the New World. Still hoping to find a waterway that would lead to India, he searched the shores of the Caribbean.

Word reached Montezuma that great birds had been seen floating on the sea, carrying men with red beards and faces white as chalk. Then they had flown away.

But they would return. Montezuma knew that they would return, those white and bearded men. And Quetzalcoatl would be with them. The time was here. The Feathered Serpent was coming to defeat his brother, to reconquer this high valley, and to rebuild his ruined temple.

Montezuma knew that he and his empire were doomed. And indeed they were. The conqueror was coming. He was almost there. Not Quetzalcoatl, but a young, bearded Spaniard by the name of Cortez was to conquer the Aztecs.

Tenochtitlán, the Aztec city, would be destroyed. On its ruins, Mexico City would be built, the first great Spanish city in the New World.

INDEX

Numbers in italics refer to maps.

Fourteen Hundred
Ninety Two
Columbus
sailed
the Ocean blue
1492
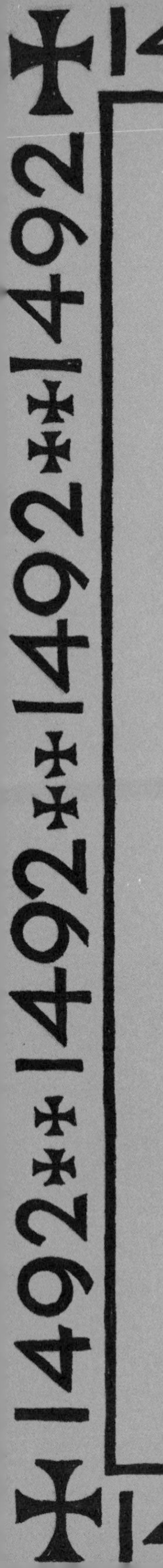

1492**1492**1492
Fourteen Hundred
Ninety Two
Columbus
sailed
the Ocean blue
1492
1492**1492**1492